JUST WRITE IT

Tell your Story, Write your Book

Winsome Duncan

[Left Intentionally Blank]

Published by

P E A C H E S

P U B L I C A T I O N S

www.peachespublications.co.uk

[Left Intentionally Blank]

Published in London, UK by Peaches Publications, 2019.

www.peachespublications.co.uk

First Edition

ISBN: 9780955489099

British Library Cataloguing in Publication Data: A catalogue record for this book is available from the British Library.

Book cover design: Peaches Publications.

Proofreader: Joanna Oliver.

Typesetter: Winsome Duncan.

[Left Intentionally Blank]

Contents Page

Just Write It

belongs to author:

____

The Contract

I____

(insert your name above)

promise to be committed, focused and respectful of the process of writing my book and telling my story.

I understand that I need to make time to write each week and I am dedicated to achieving all my writing goals.

This contract is an agreement with myself to complete my book in the year 20____.

Signed:_____________

Date:____/____/____

Introduction

Congratulations for getting this far in your book-writing journey and taking the next step to realising your vision as a published author. It takes much courage to be set apart from the average Joe and to not only start a piece of written work but to most importantly complete it. Many people talk about how they want to write a book but for various reasons, they never get around to it. As they say, “talk is cheap”, yet it is the action and effort that you put forth into committing pen to paper and completing your manuscript that really counts.

In my experience over the past 20 years, I have learned the top 7 keys reasons why people do not complete their books. Take a look and see if any of these reasons sound familiar to you:

1. There is not enough time
2. My funds are low
3. I am lacking in motivation
4. I am a procrastinator
5. Frequent feelings of depression
6. Suffering from self-doubt
7. My laptop or PC does not work

Just Write It

Tell your Story, Write your Book

It is so sad to see many dreams of writing and completing books deferred. Do not take your book ideas and concepts to the grave, you must live what is in you and express the stories buried deep within. In my experience when working one to one with authors, the ones who complete their books have the following traits:

- Commitment
- Focus
- Dedication
- Passion
- Self-belief
- Courage
- Determination
- Faith
- Conviction
- Proactiveness

Writing a book is a serious matter, when you write a book, not only are you leaving behind your legacy for the next generation to come, you are leaving your energy signature on earth's physical plane. All the human life experience that you have amassed whilst being alive on the planet will remain in your written halls of history. Once you have made this decision, be committed, as it is your duty to see it through to the last chapter. Remember your word is your bond.

Happy writing!

What is your Why?

Can you honestly list your top 10 reasons why you want to write a book? Is it for fame and recognition? Maybe you would like to earn an extra monthly income, or you may want to go on that fabulous holiday you have been dreaming of.

It is important for you to have clarity in the direction you want your written work to go. Do you have some valuable knowledge which you would like to share with the world? Consider your why carefully and write down your truthful responses below:

1...

2...

3...

4...

5...

6...

7...

8...

9...

10..

Identifying your Writer's Avatar

Having worked with authors for many years, I have identified and created the top 4 Writer's Avatars that I encounter. Inevitably, you will fit into one of these Avatars, which will help you to understand the way in which you write and in what ways you can improve, so you can complete your book. Take a look at the descriptions and write the name of your Avatar below.

My Writer's Avatar is______________________________

The Tortoise Writer, writes at their own pace and will complete their book, when they are good and ready. Writing is a labour of love and they need to be mindful of major delays when writing.

The Perfectionist Writer

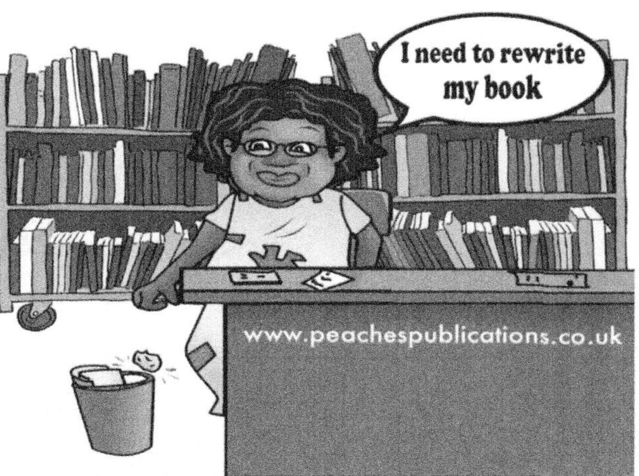

The Perfectionist Writer is in danger of not completing their book. They need to be confident that their writing is fit for purpose & publish.

The Proactive Writer

The Proactive Writer has tunnel vision when completing their book. They may be in danger of rushing their writing & would need to quality check their work periodically.

The Tomorrow Writer

The Tomorrow Writer has the best intention, but lacks commitment. They need to make a definitive decision to put pen to paper & start writing.

Choosing your Genre

More often than not, writers tend to know what types of books they would like to write. Usually, they are an expert in a particular field and they want to share their knowledge with the world. On many occasions, I hear writers want to tell their life story which is inevitably a lengthy book. I advise them to write it as a trilogy, for example segmented into sections covering child, young adult and adult. This breaks down their journey and they are more likely to complete their book in a reasonable amount of time. The following lists are created for those potential authors who have a burning desire to write but do not know what genre to go with.

Genre

Pick a genre that you know a lot about and feel confident with, as this will help you during your writing process. If you work in a school as a teacher, then you may want to write a children's book with the knowledge, wisdom and insights that you have. This means that your genre would be children's literature. If you wanted to write a book on losing weight by eating low carbs, then your genre would be health, fitness or personal-development. Selecting the correct genre for your book will be integral to your sales via Amazon distribution, make sure you choose the right category. You must label your genre correctly, do not confuse yourself with book themes, topics or subject matters.

Fiction	Non-fiction
Action and adventure	Art
Alternative history	Autobiography
Anthology	Biography
Chick lit	Book review
Children's literature	Cookbook
Comic book	Diary
Coming-of-age	Dictionary
Crime	Encyclopaedia
Drama	Guide
Fairy-tale	Health
Fantasy	History
Graphic novel	Journal
Historical fiction	Math
Horror	Memoir
Mystery	Prayer
Paranormal romance	Religion, new age and spirituality
Picture book	Textbook
Poetry	Review
Political thriller	Science
Romance or erotica romance	Self help
Satire	Travel
Science fiction	True crime
Short story	Self – development
Suspense	Fitness
Thriller – Young adult	

99 Writing Themes

Choosing your Themes

Now you know the category of your genre and for this example, we are using children books. You must proceed to select 5 themes that match the narrative of your children's book, for example:

Empowerment

Communication

Nature

Family

Optimism

The following themes list are not exhaustive, have fun with this and be sure to select your final 5.

1. Autobiography
2. Birthing
3. Capitalism – effect on the individual
4. Change versus tradition
5. Chaos and order
6. Character – destruction, building up
7. Circle of life
8. Coming of age
9. Communication – verbal and nonverbal
10. Companionship
11. Convention and rebellion
12. Dangers of ignorance

13. Darkness and light
14. Death – inevitable or tragedy
15. Depression
16. Desire to escape
17. Dictatorship
18. Disillusionment and dreams
19. Displacement
20. Economics
21. Empowerment
22. Emptiness of attaining false dream
23. Everlasting love
24. Facing darkness
25. Facing reality
26. Fading beauty (ageing)
27. Faith versus doubt
28. Fashion
29. Famine
30. Family
31. Fate and free will
32. Fear of failure
33. Female roles
34. Fulfilment
35. Good versus evil
36. Greed as downfall
37. Growing up
38. Governments
39. Hazards of passing judgment
40. Heartbreak of betrayal
41. Heroism – real and perceived
42. Hierarchy in nature
43. Identity crisis
44. Illness
45. Illusion of power
46. Immortality
47. Inner versus outer strength
48. Injustice

49. Isolation
50. Knowledge versus ignorance
51. Loneliness as destructive force
52. Losing hope
53. Loss of innocence
54. Lost honour
55. Lost love
56. Love and sacrifice
57. Man against nature
58. Manipulation
59. Materialism
60. Mental health
61. Motherhood
62. Music
63. Names – power and significance
64. Nationalism
65. Nature
66. Necessity of work
67. Oppression of women
68. Optimism – power or folly
69. Overcoming – fear, weakness, vice
70. Patriotism – positive side or complications
71. Plastic surgery
72. Power and corruption
73. Power of words
74. Pride and downfall
75. Progression
76. Quest for discovery of self
77. Quest for power
78. Racism
79. Rebirth
80. Reunion
81. Role of men
82. Role of Religion – virtue or hypocrisy
83. Role of women
84. Self-awareness

85. Self-preservation
86. Self-reliance
87. Social mobility
88. Society
89. Technology in society
90. Temptation and destruction
91. Traditions
92. Vanity
93. Vulnerability
94. Virgin brides
95. War
96. Will to survive
97. Wisdom of experience
98. Working class struggles
99. Youth and beauty

Selecting the Correct Book Title and Subtitle

Did you know that fiction is the bestselling genre of books on Amazon? Following that is 'number books', for example, 100 Ways to Cook an Egg and 'how-to' books are also bestselling on Amazon. Guess how many copies of their book an author will sell in its lifetime? The answer will be revealed at the end of this chapter. When selecting a title, it must stand out from all the other books and be catchy. Please remember these are working titles and working subtitles and you do not have to choose a final title/subtitles straight away. Let your book speak to you as you write, you will innately know what the final title should be. Explore some ideas below:

Working Titles

1...

2...

3...

4...

5...

A subtitle is a secondary book title which serves as a wider description of the book content, for example:

Title: 100 Ways to Cook an Egg

Subtitle: Using a Halogen Cooker

Now the reader understands that if they have a gas cooker, this book is not for them.

Working Subtitles

1...

2...

3...

4...

5...

Final Title

....

Final Subtitle

....

Answer: *The general life of book sales is 300 sold copies.* Authors normally tend to recoup their publishing expenses only. In order to make a profit you must use our media press kit and six months marketing strategy to maximise sales.

Industry Standard Table of Contents Page

Please make sure that your book has our suggested 'industry standard' table of contents (TOC). Some book subject matters may not need all the content inserts, choose appropriately or ask for advice. This page will be located at the beginning of your book, after the legal page. Leave a blank page between your legal page and table of contents.

Dedication
This section is intended to thank a person or persons who supported or influenced you to write your book. They can be living or dead and one or two sentences is enough. Any more sentences are to be considered for inclusion in the acknowledgement page.

Acknowledgements
This is to acknowledge those, in depth, who have helped you in your book writing journey or with your life experiences. For example, your spouse, children or even your book publisher and Book Confidence Consultant!

Foreword (recommended)
Written by a celebrity, someone in your industry or who has a direct relationship to you, the author. The purpose of this endorsement is usually to help you to sell more books.

Preface or Introduction

This is an introduction to the book, where you will have an opportunity to give a book overview. Decide if you want to call this section the preface or introduction, as this is merely a matter of preference.

Chapters

Chapters are there to serve as navigation for the reader.
→→→ Insert your chapter heading 1 here.
→→→ Insert your chapter heading 2 here.
→→→ Insert your chapter heading 3 here.
And so forth.

Subheadings (optional)

A subheading describe subsections of your book, which can be embodied in the body interior and contents page. They serve as a purpose to explain what you are about to read next.

Epilogue

A section at the end of a book, which serves as a conclusion to what has been written throughout the book.

About the Author

This is a mini-biography which tells your readers about who you are and what you do. You can have this section with or without a picture, it is optional. However, for identification purposes and publicity, we recommend you have a professional picture inserted in this section of your book.

Services (optional)
This is an opportunity to promote and upsell your services or products, directly to your readers. This is usually for people in business or creatives.

Reference list (optional)
If you have used quotes from other authors or reference to legal documents and other written works, you will need to credit the source or author in the body of the text interior. Use brief descriptions only and do not plagiarize their content by using large chunks of their work. Amazon Kindle has a detector and if plagiarism is found, they will delete your book.

Useful Links (optional)
These links are for your reader to gain further knowledge and insight into you book subject matter

Study Notes (optional)
For readers to make notes, when reading. Study notes are normally used for workbooks.

Chapter Headings

At Peaches Publications, we always recommend as a general rule of thumb, new authors should write a book that has:

- 100 pages
- Approximately 10,000 words
- Ten chapter headings

The reason behind this is so that our authors can set realistic and attainable targets for themselves. This is defined as a short book; however, it is achievable for the author to complete. Here are some guidelines for you to follow when deciding how long you want your book to be:

Short books: 7,000 to 20,000 words

Medium books: 20,000 to 55,000 words

Long books: 55,000 to 100,000 words

This section on chapter headings, is a chance for you to explore all your chapter ideas and concepts, via creative thinking. Even if you think a chapter heading sounds silly, I want you to write it down. Be sure to fill in both pages, this will enable you to have a wide selection to choose from when selecting your final ten chapter headings.

Sample Chapter Headings

Chapter ....

Chapter ....

Chapter ....

Chapter ....

Chapter ....

Chapter ....

Chapter ....

Chapter ....

Chapter ....

Chapter ....

Chapter ....

Chapter ....

Chapter ....

Chapter ....

Chapter ....

Chapter ....

Chapter ....

Chapter ....

Chapter ....

Sample Chapter Headings

Chapter ....

Chapter ....

Chapter ....

Chapter ....

Chapter ....

Chapter ....

Chapter ....

Chapter ....

Chapter ....

Chapter ....

Chapter ....

Chapter ....

Chapter ....

Chapter ....

Chapter ....

Chapter ....

Chapter ....

Chapter ....

Chapter ....

Final Ten Chapter Headings

(All chapters must be in consecutive order.)

Chapter 1………………………………………………………………

Chapter 2………………………………………………………………

Chapter 3………………………………………………………………

Chapter 4………………………………………………………………

Chapter 5………………………………………………………………

Chapter 6………………………………………………………………

Chapter 7………………………………………………………………

Chapter 8………………………………………………………………

Chapter 9………………………………………………………………

Chapter 10……………………………………………………………

Story Framework Overview

Sometimes writing a book can feel overwhelming, especially If you are in a full-time job plus have a family, with very little time to spare. We have made this workbook as simple as possible, to help you to write efficiently and effectively. You now need to create a brief book outline to establish the direction of your manuscript, creating a roadmap for completing your book will help you to finish quicker. You can write a paragraph or make bullet points in the following sections, to plot your book sequences. This is not a lengthy task, use it as a navigation map for your book and for making your ideas more concise. Your story framework should serve as a brief overview of the contents of your entire book.

Story Framework Planner

Beginning

Middle

End

Book Cover Design

In order to make your book come alive and feel real, you must use the important tool of visualisation. Now that you have selected your title and your subtitle, please spend some time thinking about what you want your book cover to look like. Go onto www.amazon.co.uk to research other books in the genre you are writing about. Type into the search bar, similar subject areas and see what books come up and use that research to develop your book cover design artwork.

Using a pencil, please sketch out two different concepts of your ideas for the book cover design. Create an account with www.canva.com and create two free book covers. Please note that you will need a professional cover designed, for your book to stand out in the competitive Amazon market. When I work with an author, we complete a book cover design form and have a consultation, as it is crucial to get this part of the publishing process correct. The purpose of this exercise is to use your book covers as your muse and a source of inspiration to finish your book.

The minute you add pen to paper or type your first word, I want you to acknowledge you have become an author, irrespective of whether your book is finished. Say it and believe it from the crown of your head to the soles of your feet. Feel the energy of your completed book in your aura, on a daily basis and it shall come to pass.

Please note, if you are publishing with Peaches Publications, your book cover will be subject to change. This is because we have our own processes in making a cover design and we support our authors in this with a consultation.

Book Cover Design 1

Book Cover Design 2

Back Cover Blurb

When writing the content for the blurb that goes onto the back cover of your book, remember, this is what your potential buyer will see at first glance. Your prospect must get a sense of what the book is about, in one or two succinct paragraphs and no more. It is your opportunity to convey to your prospective reader why this book is for them and why they should purchase it from you. Things you can mention in the blurb are:

- Themes
- Content
- Benefits
- Features
- Selected chapter headings

Write down your blurb, including 100 words or less for your back cover blurb.

Back Cover Blurb

Primary and Secondary Readership

It is important to think about the person or people who will be your primary customer when buying your book. For example, if you wrote a book about the black holocaust, interested parties in buying this book would be cultural studies students, historians and university lecturers. Your secondary reader would be family members or friends who want to support you and purchase your book however, will probably never read it.

Primary Readership

Secondary Readership

Identifying your Target Readership

When you write a book, even when the subject matter is about your life's works or story, you must always have the reader in mind. They are your buyer, prospect or a potential client, so you must be clear about the narrative you want to get across. These readers are the ones who will purchase your book, which means that writing your book is not about self-gratification but about really tuning into what your reader wants. See some real-life examples of authors we have worked with, to define what their readership should be.

Target Readership	Book Content
Parents who are recently bereaved.	The author writes a book about how she coped after her daughter's suicide.
Female ethnic minorities in the corporate workplace.	The author writes a book about her personal experience of racism in corporate England.
Church ministries.	The author writes a collection of poetry to inspire Christians in their walk with Jesus Christ.
Helping families to become financially literate.	The author writes a book about managing money and improving personal finances.

Now it is time to write down your targeted reader's profile. The purpose of this task is to know what characteristics your readers have and how you can place your book in front of them and get onto the Amazon 100 bestseller's list. To build a well-rounded profile you must include:

- Race
- Class
- Age
- Demographics
- Marital status
- Social hangouts
- Magazines or newspapers they read
- Where they shop for food and clothes
- Do they have children and if yes how many?

Sample Target Reader Profile

Rosie is married to Derek. They have two daughters aged 15 and 19 years. Rosie's family is middle class, Derek works in a bank in Canary Wharf and they live in Buckinghamshire. Rosie is a black female, aged 43 years and is a stay at home mother and is now wanting to start a part-time business to counteract being bored at home. In the evenings and some weekends when she is home, Rosie likes to read Vogue, O magazine and her favourite newspaper is The Sunday Times. Rosie shops in organic food stores, Sainsbury's, Waitrose, Selfridges and makes regular online purchases. Rosie loves to attend networking events, conferences, seminars, business brunches and weekend spas with her daughters and close friends.

Your Target Reader Profile

The 24-Hour Formula

Writing a book is a very intimate, private process. It requires you to go deep within and write out your deepest thoughts from your invisible world. Please pay close attention to what I am about to say next, as many pay thousands of pounds for this formula; I am going to share our top industry secret with you! Are you ready?

This secret is the master key to completing your book in a short space of time and getting it ready for print. This knowledge is just for you because you took the time to invest in your dream of being an author. Listen to me closely, how you write a book using 'The 24-Hour Formula' is..........................

1 Audio record your book and get it transcribed.

Or

2 Use voice dictation on your computer to type for you.

These two tips offer budding authors some revolutionary information, yet sadly many do not do this and potentially their book never gets completed. Please note that how you speak is how the transcriber will type your book, always use standard English and use an Editor to develop your audio into a comprehensive text.

If you decide upon number one, then you can hire a transcriber on www.upwork.com. This knowledge is what you paid for, it sounds simple enough, right? However, unless you are in the book writing industry, others are unwilling to share these precious writing secrets with you. Peaches Publications also offer a transcribing service if you wish to compare quotes.

The 24-Hour Formula

The 24-Hour Formula is based on a 30-day turnaround of your book. Once the core of your book is written, you can then go back to edit and tweak your manuscript. We recommend editing after your book has been written, as we do not want you to be hindered by the writing process. Please select a model that best suits your time schedule and stick to it, for consistency.

Model One
Select 3 consecutive days where you will sit down and write or record for up to 8 hours. Most authors book a weekend break-away in a hotel to accomplish this. This model is the quick version to completing and re-reading your book with the 24-hour timeframe. It is the most intensive model.
Model Two
Write 2 hours per day. You must write content 5 days out of 7 per week. In your third week, you will have achieved your 24 hours. After this time, you can go back and edit your manuscript as a whole document and prepare it for pre-publication.
Model Three
This model is working over a 30-day period. Write consecutively for 1 hour per day for the next 24 days. Mornings are the best for this, before anyone gets up in your household. The last 6 days should be dedicated to a read through and edit, where you can tweak your book to the final version.

Do's and Don'ts

Here are some suggestions of my very own private do's and don'ts when writing my books and which I share with my author-clients.

Do's

- Switch off phones when writing, or at the very minimum switch it to silent. Make sure that you cannot hear your phone vibrating, as it is a mental distraction. Interruption from electrical devices breaks the flow in concentration when writing and it takes 11 minutes to reset yourself and refocus upon the manuscript.
- In order to keep the mind fresh and alert, take regular breaks from writing. I suggest a 2-hour block of writing and a 15-minute break. I must admit I sometimes find it hard, as I could do a 6-hour block with no breaks and be fully immersed, however, I have learned to be kinder and nurture myself in better ways, to avoid burn out or exhaustion when writing. Be sure to schedule in time for lunch, of at least 60 minutes.
- Be focused on the writing content only. Editing will come later on. Many writers make the mistake of editing their work during the creative process; this is INCORRECT! When you jump from being a writer to editor, to proof-reader, you

are really disturbing the flow of your work. Balance is integral. Work on completing the book content first and edit later.

- Do make time for writing, even if it means getting up one or two hours earlier, before the rest of your household wakes up. This is instrumental in completing your book when supposedly there is "no time to write". It is called sacrifice. I have worked with a single mother of two sons who writes her book from 10 p.m. to 2 a.m., goes to sleep and then in the morning, gets ready for work. You can make time, if you are determined.

Don'ts

- Don't try to edit your manuscript when writing content, this is a very bad habit that perfectionists have. Just enjoy the flow of writing until your book is complete. So what if there are spelling mistakes.

- Avoid repetition and use a thesaurus, to vary your language. If you are writing a book about business, the actual word 'business' may appear several times. Examples of an alternative word for 'business', to avoid repetition are:

- Company
- Work

- Corporate
- Firm
- Organisation

- Write in silence. Do not tell anyone that you are writing a book unless they are your accountability partner. When you put your book in progress into the public or social media arena, you are setting yourself up to fail. Your network will now have a huge expectation of you and may ask questions or give negative feedback. They may say, "Where is this book you are talking about?" Learn to write in silence and surprise them with a book launch invitation.

Daily Writing Planner

The following are daily planners for you to schedule your private writing time. Find a regular writing location, where you can complete your daily writing tasks, for example, researching a topic. Once you become organised, you will get used to writing frequently. It takes 21 days to make a habit, give yourself a good length of time to create a new way of connecting with your writing and be patient with yourself. Remember to photocopy your planner if you are working on your book for longer than the 3-day intensive.

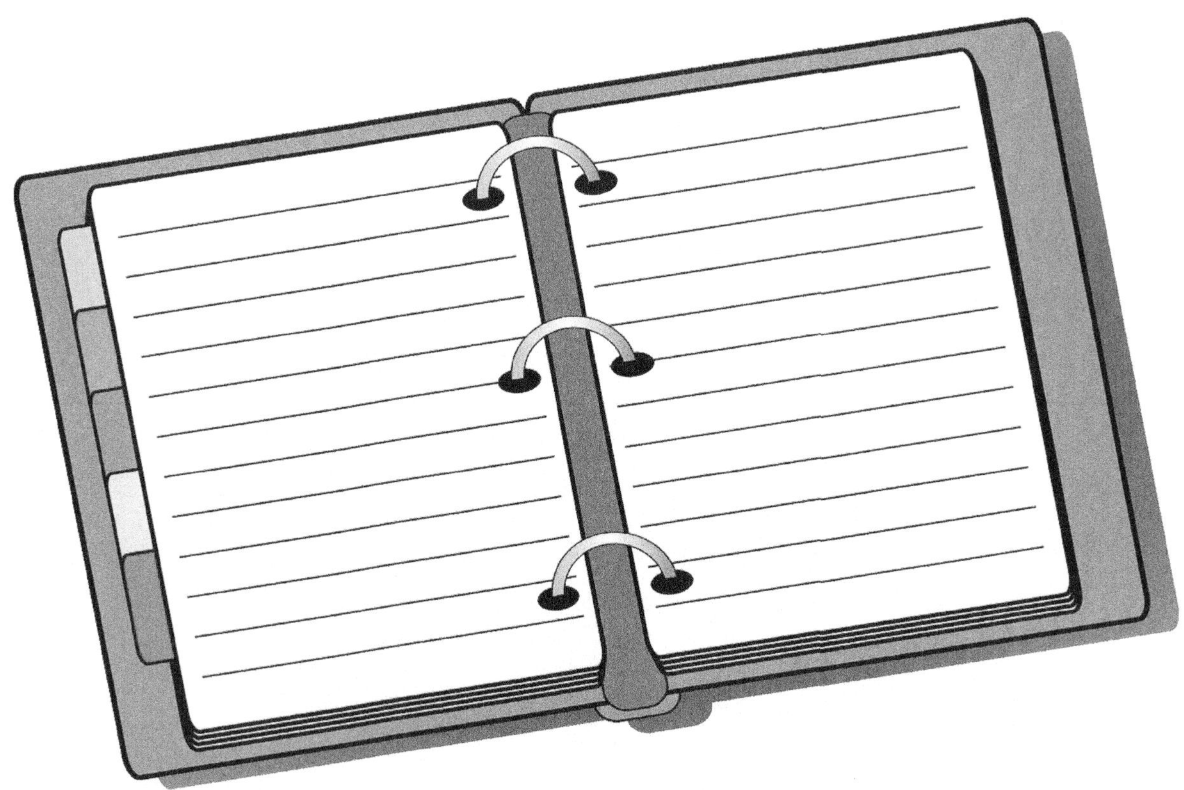

Monday Daily Tasks	
Time frame	
Morning	
Afternoon	
Evening	

Tuesday Daily Tasks	
Time frame	
Morning	
Afternoon	
Evening	

Wednesday Daily Tasks	
Time frame	
Morning	
Afternoon	
Evening	

Thursday Daily Tasks	
Time frame	
Morning	
Afternoon	
Evening	

Friday Daily Tasks	
Time frame	
Morning	
Afternoon	
Evening	

Saturday Daily Tasks	
Time frame	
Morning	
Afternoon	
Evening	

Sunday Daily Tasks	
Time frame	
Morning	
Afternoon	
Evening	

Committing Pen to Paper

Now you have arrived at the title of this book, this chapter is what your writing journey thus far has been all about, from here on, I am advising you to simply, **"Just Write It..."** Write the wrongs of the world, write for every boy and girl, write the portrait of your culture. Tell the epic story of your life. Stay focused on the writing path. There is a purpose within your pain; use your experience to heal and to teach others how to live their best life.

Writing is such a cathartic release and it can help free the reader of their invisible shackles and bondage they carry on a daily basis. Write to capture the story of your time on planet earth, leave a legacy and shine brightly forever. Spread your word far and wide and make sure your message is heard by the masses. Think global domination!

Writing a literary text is a sign of the times that things are changing; a change *must* come, we have to change, let us be the change we want to see in the world. This is your opportunity to give a voice to the muted stories or poetic verses whirling around in your head; so budding authors, write without ceasing! Write as passionately as the breath you breathe into your lungs. If you follow the directives given to you in this book, you will pick up your words and pen and tell the stories of the ages, one day at a time. Simply put: Just Write It.

Just Write It....

Your next task is to simply JUST WRITE IT...

Just Write It

Just Write It

Just Write It

Just Write It

Just Write It

Just Write It

Just Write It

Just Write It

Just Write It

Writer's Block

This exercise is to help you with writer's block. Do this as often as you can in order to break through any barriers to writing. You must use a pen and paper for this exercise. It does not matter what comes to mind or how strange your thoughts are, even it is to write that the walls are green and the carpet is red. Just go with the flow and write without ceasing. The aim here is to push past the fluff of words that are getting in the way of you writing your story.

Writer's Block Free Flow Exercise

For the next 5 minutes without ceasing, write down everything that comes to your mind.

Writer's Block Free Flow Exercise

For the next 15 minutes without ceasing, write down everything that comes to your mind.

Writer's Block Free Flow Exercise

For the next 30 minutes without ceasing, write down everything that comes to your mind.

Epilogue

My wish for you, when you start writing your book, is that you simply finish it. With focus, discipline and determination, you can do this, I believe in you.

The reason we use blank pages rather than lined paper, is to allow us to be free with our writing. Lined and uniformed pages are so rigid and can prevent you from finding your freedom of expression. I also advise that you purchase an A5 notebook to capture your ideas and concepts about your book, that may not all necessarily fit in this workbook.

Back in the day, when I was not as busy as I am now, I used to write freehand on paper and then type it up. There is something about your energy signature, which is left on the page; writing in this manner is organic and is a somewhat 'luxurious' way of writing. Choose an approach that works best for you and remember, if you need additional one-to-one Book Confidence Consultancy, you can send me an email request.

Good luck with completing your book and do let me know how you are getting on with your book writing and share any questions you have at wepublish@peachespublications.co.uk.

Warmest regards,

Winsome Duncan

About the Author

Winsome Duncan - Book Confidence Consultant

Meet the award-winning entrepreneur and Founder of Peaches Publications, Winsome Duncan. Her book publishing experience spans more than a decade and she is passionate about books. Winsome is a bestselling author with ten books in her repertoire.

Winsome's written television work has featured on BBC iPlayer, SKY, Virgin TV and BBC London radio. As a motivational speaker, Winsome was trained by the renowned multi-millionaire and motivational speaker, Les Brown and has trained with the UK's top speaker, Andy Harrington.

Her books are highly acclaimed, having received national press and media coverage and Winsome has been endorsed by former Minister of Justice, Sir Simon Hughes.

Winsome's book publishing specialisms are:

- Editing
- Proofreading
- Ghost Writing
- Book Cover Design
- Copyright Protection
- Kindle Digital Upload

Just Write It

Tell your Story, Write your Book

- Book Confidence Consulting
- Amazon Distribution Channels
- Paperback and Hardback Books
- Critical Friend Manuscript Analysis
- Book Structure Assessment and Analysis

For expertise in your inbox, sign up for Peaches Publications newsletters, here: www.peachespublications.co.uk.

BEST
amazon.com
SELLER

Printed in Great Britain
by Amazon

37184584R00046